IMAGES
of America

MARSHALL
COUNTY

FROM THE COLLECTION OF
CHESLEY THORNE SMITH

IMAGES
of America

MARSHALL
COUNTY
FROM THE COLLECTION OF
CHESLEY THORNE SMITH

Mary Carol Miller

ARCADIA
PUBLISHING

ISBN 978-1-5316-4531-1

Published by Arcadia Publishing
Charleston SC, Chicago IL, Portsmouth NH, San Francisco CA

Library of Congress Catalog Card Number: Applied for

For all general information contact Arcadia Publishing at:
Telephone 843-853-2070
Fax 843-853-0044
E-mail sales@arcadiapublishing.com
For customer service and orders:
Toll-Free 1-888-313-2665

Visit us on the Internet at www.arcadiapublishing.com

Contents

ACKNOWLEDGMENTS

Several years ago, while writing a book on Mississippi's historic architecture, I had the pleasure of meeting and working with Chesley Thorne Smith. My early inquiries into the long-vanished mansions of Marshall County all led me to Chesley, known throughout the community for her extensive and well-catalogued collection of photographs. When she decided to publish this collection, I was quite honored that she contacted me to assist her. Though the words of the captions may be mine, the memories and the life in these photos are all hers. The hours we spent in her basement "fileroom," reliving the days captured so eloquently by her camera, allowed me a glimpse into a time and place that she has preserved forever. Holly Springs is much richer for Chesley's life having been spent there, and I cannot begin to express my gratitude for her willingness to share that life with me and the readers of this book.

I am also very much indebted to two men who provided much of the historical detail and background for this project. Dr. Hubert McAlexander, professor of English at the University of Georgia, is a native of Holly Springs whose heart obviously remains there. His knowledge of the history and lore of Marshall County never fails to amaze me, and I am most grateful for his willingness to proofread and correct the factual errors of my rough drafts. Dr. Milton Winter, pastor of Holly Springs's First Presbyterian Church, provided me with invaluable insight through the publication of *Shadow of a Mighty Rock*, officially a history of Presbyterianism in Marshall County but actually one of the most thorough and beautifully written local histories I have ever read. Its wealth of detail on all aspects of early Holly Springs life provided much of the background for my text, and I would strongly recommend his book for anyone interested in further research on this part of Mississippi.

Finally, my thanks go to all the gracious people of Holly Springs and Marshall County, who live and breathe Southern hospitality every day, and to my husband and children, who have come to understand why Holly Springs keeps calling me back.

INTRODUCTION

Tucked just under the Tennessee-Mississippi line, only 30 minutes from the suburban sprawl of Memphis, is a time capsule: Marshall County and Holly Springs, a community where the past is revered and ever present. Mississippi's history was written in towns such as this, but most cannot begin to boast of the charm found in this town of some 7,500 people. Stand on the courthouse square and look around: The buildings lining the streets are all but unchanged from a century ago. Cover the roads with dirt and fire up some gas lamps and you could easily imagine yourself in a bustling cotton center of the 1840s.

Mississippi was a young state, just 15 years into its destiny, when the 1832 Treaty of Pontotoc heralded dramatic change. The Chickasaw Indians were relinquishing their tribal lands to the American government, kicking off a land rush that would see the population of north Mississippi explode. Thousands of virgin acres were suddenly available for rock-bottom prices, and wealthy planters in the old Atlantic states sent their sons and agents into the new territory with blank checks. Cotton prices were high and this land was ready-made for white gold. Settlers and speculators poured into the region, and towns sprang up to meet their needs.

One of the more optimal town sites developed around a spring shaded by a grove of holly trees. A tavern built nearby was an immediate success, and settlers began to construct simple dogtrot cabins and clapboard stores in the region. By 1836, Holly Springs had grown into a local trade center with some 4,000 citizens, and plans were being laid for a courthouse square and a courthouse suitable for the conduct of government. On July 6, 1836, this log building hosted the first meeting of the governing "Board of Police." They wasted no time in setting into motion a more formal replacement for a county which was so obviously on the move.

Many of Marshall County's pioneers arrived from the old cotton states of Georgia, Virginia, and the Carolinas flush with inheritances, but even those who appeared with little but the clothes on their backs found the fertile soil to be a source of ready riches. As cotton established its dominance, businesses and services opened around the square to provide an outlet for spending that money. In 1837, Holly Springs could boast of 20 dry goods stores, 2 drugstores, 3 banks, several hotels, and more than enough saloons. Two newspapers were chock-full of advertisements, and 40 lawyers kept the halls of the brand-new two-story brick courthouse quite busy.

Prosperity brought a desire for a higher standard of living than could be found in a log cabin or a dogtrot. Greek Revival styling was sweeping the country in the 1830s and 1840s, and Marshall Countians would build these domestic temples with a vengeance. The columns and formal porticoes of Oakleigh, Montrose, and the Craft-Fort-Daniel House gave way to the more fanciful styling of Cedarhurst and Airliewood, Gothic showplaces unrivaled anywhere in Mississippi.

The collapse of the cotton market in the late 1840s was only a temporary impediment in Holly Springs's march to prosperity; it rebounded to become the most prolific cotton-producing county in the state of Mississippi. Academies were established for the education of the town's children, and all the major denominations built fine church buildings, several of which are still standing and serving their congregations today. The Jones and McElwain Foundry, just north of town, manufactured elaborate ironwork which was shipped throughout the South. To all appearances, the future of Holly Springs and Marshall County was unlimited. But storm clouds were brewing, with heated rhetoric coming out of Jackson and Charleston and Washington.

Those clouds burst with a fury over north Mississippi with the onset of the Civil War; probably no town in Mississippi suffered more grievously and repeatedly than Holly Springs. From the time of its occupation by Federal forces and designation as a supply depot, the war raged on Holly Springs's doorstep for the remainder of the war. No less than 62 raids, perpetrated by first one side and then the other, drove townspeople into their homes in fear and misery. The foundry was burned and mansions were commandeered as headquarters for Union officers. When the battles finally ended, Reconstruction found a shattered populace slowly piecing together a society and economy in ruins.

As life in Marshall County returned to some semblance of normalcy, the square was rebuilt and the cotton gins once again hummed with life in the fall. But tragedy was not yet through with Holly Springs. In 1878, believing their location to be a barrier to the miasmal scourge of yellow fever, the city fathers invited refugees from hard-hit Grenada to take shelter in their town. Within days, the first Marshall County victims succumbed to the ravages of the quick and deadly plague; before the fall's first frost brought relief, over 1,400 cases of the fever were reported, with at least 300 dead.

Despite war, pestilence, and soil that was gradually diminishing in fertility, Holly Springs and Marshall County persevered and survived. Slavery gave way to a system of sharecropping that was oftentimes just as cruel; two world wars and the Great Depression took many of the townspeople away in search of a different life. One by one, the cotton gins closed and bales of cotton no longer lined the streets in the fall. Industry came to fill a more significant role in the economy, and mechanization slowly but surely eliminated all but a handful of agricultural jobs. Holly Springs retains its antebellum charm, attracting thousands to the annual Spring Pilgrimage of homes and providing a glimpse into a time that will not come again.

In researching the history of Marshall County, the Craft, Fort, and Daniel family names are woven into every corner of the fabric of this community. Hugh Craft arrived in Holly Springs when it was hardly more than a tavern stop in the wilderness, and he built the gracious Greek Revival home now known as the Craft-Fort-Daniel House. It was in this house that his great-great-granddaughter, Chesley Thorne Smith, was born in 1910. Growing up in the old house, surrounded by relatives and neighbors who carried the heritage of Holly Springs in their bearing, she soaked up the lore and legend of Marshall County, seemingly never forgetting a face or a fact. Photography was an early hobby; from 1919 on, anyone who would stand still long enough to pose became the subject of her attention, along with houses and cotton scenes and, in her words, "anything that I knew wouldn't be around much longer." Thanks to her foresight and artistic talent, we have a vast and varied record of Holly Springs throughout the twentieth century, a treasure trove that would have been lost had she not captured it for us on film.

Adding to the value of her own photographs are the many older prints and negatives which Chesley collected through the years. The pre-1900 glass negatives of Lem Johnson were carefully preserved and reproduced, throwing open a window to the past with remarkable clarity. And, happily for posterity, Chesley has been a model of organization; her filing cabinets reveal meticulously labeled files, each overflowing with images and memories of her hometown. From daguerreotypes and cyanotypes of faces which witnessed civil war and yellow fever, right up to the modern sights of homecoming convertibles circling the square, her collection is a truly unique reflection of a century and a half in one enduring Mississippi community.

One

THE HEART OF
HOLLY SPRINGS

The center and soul of Marshall County for 160 years has been the Holly Springs square. Dominated by the Greek Revival courthouse, it has endured as an economic hub, seemingly oblivious to the outlying development which has doomed so many other downtowns to decay. This same site saw the first government building for the fledgling county erected in 1838; that structure stood until Union troops accidentally set it on fire in 1864, bringing down the domed octagonal cupola and copper roof that had been such a source of pride to a booming frontier town.

The core of the present-day courthouse was a Reconstruction project, completed in 1870 by the architectural firm of Willis, Sloan, and Trigg. Major renovations of 1929 altered it to essentially the building seen today.

The businesses which line the square have changed names through the years, but many of the buildings date back to the earliest days of Holly Springs. The south side is the oldest of the four, while the original north and east facades were destroyed in the daring Confederate raid of 1862.

Cotton bales line the roads around the courthouse in this turn-of-the-century photo. The elaborate iron fence circling the courthouse grounds was erected in October 1870, paid for by a one-mill tax. In 1927, as autos began to outnumber horses as a means of transportation in Holly Springs, the hitching posts were declared expendable and the fence was dismantled. Mr. and Mrs. Robert Tyson purchased it for $300 and placed it around their home.

This view of the courthouse was taken from the southeast corner of the square. With five gins running full-blast each fall, cotton bales were piled along every available thoroughfare. Children looked forward to the yearly ritual of hopping along the bales on their way to and from school each day.

This glass negative print shows Market Street facing north, c. 1900. The north and east sides of the square were rebuilt after being destroyed in General Van Dorn's raid of December 1862. The three-story building on the right is the Masonic Hall, built in 1870. It burned in a spectacular fire in February 1951; when the blaze threatened to spread across downtown Holly Springs, firetrucks were rushed from Memphis by order of Mayor "Boss" Crump, a Holly Springs native. Note the old administration building of Rust College in the distance.

Another 1900-era glass negative captures the east side of the square. Cotton bales offered a convenient perch for watching the bustle of activity on a typical fall day. The Masonic Hall is the three-story structure; just to its right is J.G. Leach's grocery and feed store. This building later housed a hardware store owned by Chesley Smith's stepfather. Next door is Levy's, a general merchandise store founded in 1858.

This medicine show in front of the courthouse attracted a large crowd around 1900. Minstrels would appear in town with much fanfare, parading from the depot into downtown. In this era before movies, radio, and television, the songs, skits, and dances of the minstrels were a form of entertainment enjoyed by both black and white audiences. After enthralling the townspeople with music and comedy, the "patent medicine" salesman would make his pitch for a wonder elixir, guaranteed to cure most any ailment which might plague the citizens of Marshall County.

Sheep kick up a cloud of dust as they are driven through one of the streets just off the square, an indication of just how agrarian Holly Springs was as the twentieth century dawned. To the right is the Baptist Church; the back of the Masonic Lodge can be seen in the distance.

Postcards of local scenes were extraordinarily popular in the early 1900s. This one pictured a busy day on the square in Holly Springs; no indication is given as to whether this was a special occasion or just a typical business day.

This photograph of the Marshall County Courthouse shows its original 1870 design. The heavy brackets underneath the eaves and the tall, arched windows are elements of Italianate styling; the formal portico with Corinthian columns is typical of the Greek Revival influence still so popular in Southern architecture.

The courthouse underwent extensive renovation and expansion in 1929–1930. Many of the original decorative elements were removed and two large wings were added to the east and west sides. This photo from the 1950s shows essentially the same building which stands today.

Two

COTTON KINGDOM

In antebellum Mississippi, cotton was truly king. Those counties with fertile soil and ready planters enjoyed a phenomenal prosperity, evidenced today by the mansions and legacies they left behind. Marshall County reigned for several of those years as the top cotton producer in the state, and the earliest photos of Holly Springs life demonstrate that this dependence on "white gold" was unchanged 50 years after the Civil War.

Thinning topsoil, the emergence of the Mississippi Delta as an agricultural powerhouse, and a more diversified economy have all but eliminated cotton as a staple of Marshall County's daily life. The sounds of gin machinery clattering throughout the night, once the lullaby for Holly Springs's children, are just a fading memory. The autumn air is no longer filled with wisps of loose cotton drifting off the packed wagons, and youngsters don't hop to school along massive bales lining the streets. This time is gone, but certainly not forgotten; Chesley Smith's photographic collection documents every aspect of producing a cotton crop, from long, hot days in the fields to the festive atmosphere on the square as King Cotton rolled through in its annual parade to the gins.

Sometime around 1900, a sharecropper fills a basket with cotton; most farmers remained in the fields from August to December in a backbreaking race to harvest as much cotton as possible from each acre.

Decades later, the same labor-intensive nature of cotton kept entire families in the fields for weeks. Children were often kept out of school until the crops were in; this young boy is attempting to lift a sack of cotton, probably weighing nearly as much as he does, onto a scale for credit.

16

One of the treats of growing up in the South was playing in the cotton wagons. Filled to the brim with soft, clean bolls, a wagon with a load of cotton was the perfect venue for jumping and rolling without risk of injury.

Dated August 1939, this photo shows a family driving a wagonload of baled cotton from the gin; until World War II, mule- and horse-drawn wagons were still a common sight on the streets of Holly Springs.

This turn-of-the-century picture shows a manual cotton press, possibly powered by horse or mule. Notice the vertical screw which would drive boards together, compressing the loose cotton into a bale. Such crude presses were soon replaced by more efficient steam and electric compresses.

Each fall found Mississippi towns crowded with cotton wagons on the way to the gins and massive loads of baled cotton ready to be shipped to market. In this photo from Chesley Smith's collection, an adventurous gentleman has a lofty perch on the summit of this valuable cargo; note the oxen pulling the wagon.

At one time, five gins were operating simultaneously in Holly Springs; from the time the first wagons rolled in during late August, the machinery ran day and night, filling the air with a fine cloud of cotton dust and lulling many a child to sleep with their rhythmic clanging.

This gin was located on College Street in Holly Springs, on the site where First State Bank now stands. Wagons were still the primary means of transporting cotton when this photo was taken in 1939.

The Holly Springs Gin Company was one of the last of these operations, located just off the square. After weeks of exhausting work picking and loading the crop, a trip to the gin provided a more relaxed atmosphere with a chance to catch up on some visiting.

Labor-intensive from the time the seed went into the ground until the last bale rolled out the doors, cotton was a hard taskmaster before the era of mechanization. These workers are pushing along a bale which likely weighs 400–500 pounds.

In the ginning process, cotton fiber was separated from the seed, which was then pressed for cottonseed oil. The fiber was compressed into bales for storage and shipment.

Mr. Kizer, a Holly Springs grocer, waits for his cotton to be weighed; many families retained farming interests even if their primary business was non-agricultural.

This *c.* 1900 photo shows the Holly Springs Compress surrounded by baled cotton. Though soil erosion was taking its toll on the fertility of Marshall County land, cotton still dominated the commerce of the region.

Baled cotton is stacked behind the Illinois Central Depot and Hotel, a landmark structure now renovated into a private home. Across the street from the depot is the building which still houses Phillips' Grocery.

Three

SIMPLER TIMES

Many of Chesley Smith's photos reflect a simpler way of life, when the rituals of washday or a harvest season set the pace for the day's activities. In those quieter years, before television and mechanization, families would labor together to accomplish whatever needed to be done to survive and produce an income. A task as basic as washing clothes required multiple steps and the blessing of a sunny day; autumn pulled thousands of laborers, young and old, into the fields to pick cotton. Those workers are gone now, replaced by massive machinery, and washday has been compressed into the time it takes to drop a load by the laundromat. But the daily routines of an all-but-vanished pace remain in these photos from a less complicated time.

In 1947, Mrs. Smith documented a typical washday in Holly Springs. Gus Smith III appears to be more interested in the contents of a well than in the washing process.

Without the aid of appliances, washing was an arduous and time-consuming process which often took an entire day.

When washing required a day outdoors, sunshine, and, hopefully, a breeze to aid the line-drying were no small blessings.

This Marshall County woman was undaunted by the rows of wash hanging behind her; she has essentially added a second set of hands by "using her head."

Each year, children eagerly awaited the production of molasses from sorghum. Sitting in a huge pile of sorghum with a farm family are Gus Smith III and Helen Thorne.

This child is feeding sorghum into the mill to be pressed into syrup; power was provided by the horse walking a continuous circular path.

As the syrup was boiled into molasses, children awaited a taste of the final product. The remainder would be bottled for sale and for use at home as a special treat over biscuits.

This 1952 fall photograph captures a family in the Chulahoma community heading to the fields for a day of picking cotton. Before widespread mechanization eliminated the need for field hands, entire families, down to the youngest children, would labor for weeks to harvest the demanding crop.

Cotton-picking was exhausting work, requiring repeated bending and stooping to reach all the bolls.

28

Four

MANSIONS OF MARSHALL COUNTY

The flush times of Marshall County's antebellum decades endowed the area with an architectural legacy unequalled in north Mississippi. Many of the early settlers arrived with their inherited riches already assured; those who landed here penniless often found wealth beyond their wildest expectations after a few years of hard work. Status in those heady years was demonstrated through brick and mortar, each palatial home having to be just a bit grander than the neighbors'. This competition fueled a building boom which peaked in the years immediately preceding the Civil War. From the simple, spare lines of the Craft-Fort-Daniel House to the overwhelming detail and elegance of Walter Place and Oakleigh, Holly Springs's streets were lined with columned showplaces and landscaped lawns. Plantations scattered about the county mirrored the cotton-generated riches of their owners, boasting such memorable homes as Strawberry Plains, Galena, and the sadly incomplete Morro Castle. Many of these mansions are only a memory, victims of fire and neglect and changing styles. Chesley Smith's foresight in recording their demise on film has provided posterity with dramatic images of the old houses in their last years.

In the photo above, young Len Marbury poses in front of Walter Place around 1904.

The most unusual and exuberant of Holly Springs's antebellum mansions is Walter Place, built in 1860 for Colonel Harvey Washington Walter. He combined the Corinthian columns and formal portico of Greek Revival with fanciful octagonal towers on each side. During the Federal occupation of Holly Springs, Mrs. Ulysses S. Grant stayed in Walter Place.

Colonel Walter died in the yellow fever epidemic of 1878; Walter Place was inherited by his daughter, Irene. She married Oscar Johnson Sr., who made a fortune in shoe manufacturing. The Johnsons hired a German landscape architect to transform the grounds of Walter Place into formal gardens, even though they used the mansion only as a vacation house. This view is from a rear stair window overlooking the grounds and the landscape architect's house.

30

The Craft-Fort-Daniel House was built by Chesley Smith's great-great-grandfather, Hugh Craft, in 1851; Chesley was the fifth generation of her family to live there. One of three homes in Holly Springs to have columns on all four sides, it remained in her family until the 1990s and is now a bed-and-breakfast inn.

This photo (c. 1875) of the Craft-Fort-Daniel House clearly shows the fanciful wrought-iron fence which still encircles the property today.

The Clapp-Fant House, also known as Oakleigh, was built in 1858 for Judge J.W. Clapp. Holly Springs lore tells of how Judge Clapp, desperately seeking sanctuary to avoid arrest by Federal forces, hid in one of the massive iron Corinthian capitals supporting his porch. In 1870, the house was bought by General Absalom Madden West, a legislative leader who was twice nominated for U.S. vice-president and who rebuilt the Mississippi Central Railroad following the war. Oakleigh, pictured here around 1901, has been well maintained throughout its history and is one of the most finely detailed antebellum mansions in Mississippi. Delicate wrought-iron balconies were probably forged at the local Jones and McElwain foundry; a sweeping circular stair fills the front hall, and an unusual oval dining room is located behind the stair hall.

Another Greek Revival showplace is Wakefield, originally known as the Wynne House. Built in 1858 for Joel E. Wynne, it differs from other Holly Springs mansions in having a flat portico. This house has exterior and interior walls 15 inches thick and was set afire during the Civil War; charred rafters in the attic attest to this incident. In 1890, the owner lost Wakefield in a poker game.

Strickland Place, one of the very first two-story houses in Marshall County, was built for Judge F.W. Huling in 1838. Long the home of Major William Strickland, it was hidden from the road by years of overgrown trees and wisteria vines. A serpentine walk lined with boxwoods led from the bullet-shaped front gate pillars to the unpainted old house. When it was demolished, the boards were numbered and stored for future use.

Montrose, now the headquarters of the Holly Springs Garden Club, was built in 1861 as a wedding present from Robert McGowan to his bride, Margaret Brooks. It features elaborate inlaid parquetry floors in the foyer and a curved stairway with niches for statuary.

The Dougherty House stood for many years at the corner of Spring Street and Van Dorn Avenue; its site is now occupied by a car wash.

The Crump Place was built in 1836 by Samuel McCorkle, the land commissioner who oversaw the sale of Chickasaw lands to Marshall County's first white settlers. It was the boyhood home of E.H. "Boss" Crump, the legendary Memphis politician. Each week for years, Mayor Crump's chauffeur would drive him home to Holly Springs for Sunday dinner with his mother at Crump Place.

Airliewood was built in 1858 by William Henry Coxe, the owner of Galena Plantation. It served as General Grant's headquarters during the occupation of Holly Springs; Union soldiers used the iron ornaments on the fence for target practice. In later years, it served as a private hospital run by a married couple, the Doctors Elliott. Airliewood is one of Mississippi's most outstanding examples of Gothic architecture. The pointed gables and carved vergeboards are characteristic features of this style, as are the tall, pointed windows. In this photo, the original gallery has been replaced by a newer one designed by Holly Springs architect W.W. Anderson.

Holly Springs's other Gothic Revival mansion is Cedarhurst, shown here around the turn of the century. It was built in 1858 for Dr. Charles Bonner, whose daughter, Sherwood (1849–1883), was a well-known Southern dialect writer and close friend of Henry Wadsworth Longfellow. It was sold to the Belk family around 1900 and has remained in that family ever since. Note the arches and gables of the Gothic style; the ironwork was most likely fashioned at the Jones and McElwain foundry.

The Magnolias was built in the late 1850s by William F. Mason. Like Airliewood and Cedarhurst, it incorporates many Gothic features in its design. This home was extensively damaged by soldiers during Federal occupation; a bayonet slash is still readily evident in the front door.

Most antebellum Holly Springs homes were not mansions, but even the more modest dwellings and cottages were finely detailed and gracious. One was the Edgar West House, where Chesley Smith's husband, Gus Smith Jr., was born in 1904. This house burned several years ago.

Mosswood, seen in this glass-negative photo, was remodeled by Fredonia Johnson Moss, granddaughter of Harvey Walter. It was built in the 1840s by Adrian Mayer, a lawyer from South Carolina, and was for many years the home of the Robert Seale family.

The Greek Revival cottage known as the Malone House was home to a Holly Springs physician for many years. Despite restoration by the Holly Springs Garden Club in the late 1930s, it was torn down in recent years. Note the elaborate ironwork between the front porch pillars.

This house still stands on the northwest corner of Gholson Avenue and Spring Street; it has been much altered from this c. 1900 view, with the porch removed and a small columned entrance added. It was once the home of Probate Judge Gordentia Waite; his sister, niece, and nephew-in-law all died here during the 1878 yellow fever epidemic.

Gray Gables was built in the 1840s as a simple two-story home; it was later altered to the popular Italianate style with arched windows, bracketed eaves, and tracery spandrels. Bohemian glass outlines the doorway.

The Knapp House, now known as Amokalea ("Place of Peace"), was built in 1857 and is a prime example of the raised-basement style seen in many antebellum houses of Marshall County. Mr. and Mrs. Knapp both succumbed to yellow fever in 1878; the home later belonged to Congressman Wall Doxey.

The Wheatley Place, once home to merchant Isaac Wheatley, still stands on Gholson Avenue in a much altered form. After suffering a fire, it was bricked and divided for apartment use.

This Greek Revival cottage, built around 1836, was the land office where Chesley Smith's great-great-grandfather worked as an agent for the American Land Company. In 1878, owner W.J.L. Holland offered it as lodging for friends fleeing the outbreak of yellow fever in Grenada; from this small house, the fever spread through Holly Springs, eventually causing over 300 deaths. Since that time, this has been known as "the Yellow Fever House." This photo shows the entrance on the south side; it was originally on the west side of the structure.

The Samuel O. Caruthers House was built in 1842. Dr. Caruthers was a first cousin of Sam Houston, and Holly Springs lore tells of several visits by the famous "Indian fighter" to the young town.

Following the devastation of Civil War and Reconstruction, Holly Springs's architectural tastes changed to mirror the exuberant Queen Anne and Second Empire styles sweeping the country. Several magnificent Victorian houses were built during this period, including this one built for merchant I.C. Levy in the 1880s. This home is still standing, much altered after a fire destroyed the second floor.

This Queen Anne cottage was located where the Merchant and Farmers' drive-in branch now stands.

The Walthall-Freeman House was the childhood home of U.S. Senator Edward Cary Walthall; his grandniece, noted artist Kate Freeman Clark, lived here after many years in New York City studying with painter William Chase. The small addition above the main entrance was a studio, since removed. Kate Clark did no painting after returning to Holly Springs and never felt that it was proper to sell her works; over 1,000 paintings were stored in New York City and later moved into the gallery which she provided for in her will. The house and gallery are now owned by the City of Holly Springs.

This Victorian cottage was for many years the home of Ella Fowler; it is located on West Chulahoma Avenue.

The Rittlemeyer House is another Victorian cottage which still stands on Randolph Street.

The Episcopal Rectory was designed by architect Samuel Patton in 1880. It features several elements of the Italianate style, including curved-arch windows and a square tower.

This elaborate towered house was home to Bishop Elias Cottrell, a leader in the Colored Methodist Episcopal Church who founded Mississippi Industrial College. His home was located on West Boundary Street.

This structure was built in 1870 as a home for Turner Lane, a Holly Springs businessman. He sold the house to the State Normal School for Negroes in 1872; it later was used as a private home for the manager of the Experiment Station. At the time that the Ames family lived there in the 1920s, blackboards remained on the walls of a huge upstairs room.

A photo prior to 1910 shows the Lizzie Tucker House, built by Captain George M. Buchanan from parts shipped from Battle Creek, Michigan. It still stands on the southwest corner of Chulahoma and Memphis Street, its appearance much different after a fire destroyed the second story.

This Victorian house on Chulahoma Avenue was built by Major Brodie Crump after the Civil War. The young ladies on horseback are the Horton sisters, who lived down the street from this home.

Several large and unusual plantation houses dotted the countryside around Marshall County. Galena was an "H"-shaped home built southwest of Holly Springs. It belonged to the Coxe family, who also built Airliewood in town. Abandoned in the 1920s with all of its furnishings remaining, it gradually deteriorated and was eventually torn down.

This small brick building was a part of the complex at Galena; it appears to be an outhouse, but, oddly enough, it was located in front of the main house.

William Blanton Lumpkin made a fortune with two huge sawmills just south of Holly Springs. When the Civil War began, he was building Morro Castle, a 22-room mansion with an enormous sandstone foundation and six Corinthian columns. War interrupted work with only one wing of the home finished; Mr. Lumpkin lived in this corner of the unfinished mansion until his death in 1877. The towering shell of a house stood empty until the 1930s, when it was demolished during the construction of Wall Doxey State Park. This mid-1930s photo shows Gus Smith and Ed Booker standing by the remains of the foundation.

Hickory Park was the 1838 Laws Hill home of Volney Peel, one of Marshall County's first settlers. It was the first brick house built out from Holly Springs and was ornamented with many fine details reminiscent of the old Atlantic Coast mansions. Abandoned after 1900, it was torn down in the 1940s.

In the 1930s, Chesley Smith braved underbrush and snakes to take detailed pictures of the remnants of Hickory Park. Notice the arched fanlight above the doorway and the Flemish bond pattern of the brickwork.

Not all of the early homes of Marshall County were gracious mansions; even more common was the simple log dogtrot exemplified by this house on the Balfour Plantation.

Strawberry Plains, about 4 miles north of Holly Springs, was built in 1851 for Colonel Ebenezer Nelms Davis. In 1865, Federal troops set fire to it and left it as a wrecked shell. This 1930s photo shows the dilapidated old home with the double line of towering cedar trees leading up to it. The home was restored in the 1970s by John and Margaret Shackleford.

During the 1850s, Major Josiah P.M. Stephenson built this story-and-a-half Greek Revival home in the tiny settlement of Mack, about 5 miles north of Holly Springs. The highway there still includes a wide, sweeping curve, designed to go around Major Stephenson's garden. This 1913 photo shows the Stephenson/McAlexander family gathered for a Christmas portrait on the front portico of the home. A similar portico is found on the rear of the house, with a brick wing incorporating a dining room and kitchen attached by a gallery. The plantation office next to the main house served for many years as the Mack post office and also as a schoolhouse. After the last inhabitants moved out in the 1970s, this house gradually deteriorated and was stripped of its mantels and hardware by vandals. It still stands today as a sad and crumbling relic.

This c. 1895 photo shows the Austin Moore House, located about 8 miles northwest of Holly Springs. Austin Moore and his brother, Henry, were two of the earliest settlers of Marshall County, and they built similar houses here and at Red Banks around 1850. The Moore House had four large rooms and a central hallway downstairs; upstairs, there were two rooms on each side, reached by separate stairs with no access between the east rooms and the west ones. This unusual arrangement was found in several other antebellum houses in north Mississippi. The home was torn down in the 1960s. Those in the picture include Pearl Kelsey (standing in shawl and cap at the fence) and young Fred Cooper (perched on the fence).

The Tyson home was a large Victorian structure owned by Mrs. Dora Alexander Tyson. She rented rooms to bachelors, and for many years this was known as "the Tyson Hotel." After Mrs. Tyson's death, her children lived in the home until the 1960s, when it was demolished.

Five

ACADEMIC CENTER OF NORTH MISSISSIPPI

Holly Springs was scarcely more than a clearing in the wilderness when plans were laid for its first school; by 1836, students were enrolling at the Holly Springs Female Institute. This was only the first in a long and illustrious series of academic institutions which would firmly establish Marshall County as a mecca for education. Schools such as Chalmers Institute, St. Thomas Hall, Bethlehem Academy, and the University of Holly Springs have long ago faded into history, but their graduates contributed in many significant ways to the state and nation. Franklin Female Institute and Malone College were evidence of Holly Springs's unique emphasis on providing educational opportunities for its young women. Mississippi Synodical College enjoyed a long and successful tenure in Holly Springs, expanding its program to educate both local primary schoolchildren and college-level coeds from across the country before merging with Jackson's Belhaven College in 1939. Rust College grew out of Reconstruction efforts to provide education and skills for recently freed slaves; it continues today as one of Mississippi's premier private colleges. Just across the road from Rust are the few remaining buildings of Mississippi Industrial College, another pioneer institution for African-American students.

The first Holly Springs Public School, pictured here, was built in 1879. It was run by Professor W.A. Anderson, former headmaster of Chalmers Institute, who spearheaded the drive for a public school system in Holly Springs. His wife, Helen Craft Anderson, was a great-great-aunt of Chesley Smith.

HOLLY SPRINGS FEMALE INSTITUTE

REV. G. W. SILL, A. M. PRINCIPAL.

Holly Springs Female Institute was the first educational institution established in Marshall County, chartered in January 1836. In 1838, the cornerstone was laid for this Greek Revival building, large enough to accommodate 140 pupils with 60 boarders. The school was in use as a hospital when it burned in 1864.

This two-story brick structure is the oldest existing academic building in north Mississippi. Originally constructed in 1837 as the Holly Springs Literary Institution, it later housed the University of Holly Springs (the first state-chartered university in Mississippi, predating Ole Miss by nine years) and then Chalmers Institute. Following the Civil War, Chalmers Institute was operated by Professor W.A. Anderson until 1869.

St. Thomas Hall was a boys' military school established in 1844 under the auspices of the Episcopal Church. After its buildings were destroyed in the Civil War, it took over the grounds of Bethlehem Academy, a Catholic school for girls. The main building was the Pointer House, an antebellum doctor's mansion.

Graduates of St. Thomas Hall included several Civil War generals, supreme court justices, a U.S. senator, and a future secretary of state. Those pictured here were members of the Class of 1898.

The stated aim of St. Thomas Hall was to "give young men Thorough, Competent and Exact Preparation for college and university work . . . along with training of the mind, the development of a strong, healthy body and a straightforward, manly Christian character." This distinguished group is the faculty and cadet officers for the 1895–96 academic year.

The antebellum mansion housing St. Thomas Hall burned during Christmas week, 1898; the school never reopened.

The most illustrious and enduring private school in Holly Springs began as Fenelon Hall, a school for young ladies founded by Elizabeth Watson in the parlor of her father's home in 1866. In its first year, it educated 15 students, including Sherwood Bonner.

By 1882, the school had expanded and was renamed Maury Institute. A large building was added behind the main house to serve boarding students. In 1888, it was endorsed by the North Mississippi Presbytery and remained under Presbyterian control throughout its existence. In 1891, Maury Institute became North Mississippi Presbyterian College (NMPC).

At NMPC, outdoor activities and exercise were encouraged; one building included an indoor swimming pool with a wooden cover to accommodate basketball and skating.

Several musical classes, including guitar, mandolin, organ, piano, and voice, were taught at NMPC. The official school publication, the *Taliaferric Journal*, identified this as the "Mandolin Class."

In addition to the college-level courses, local children could attend NMPC from kindergarten through high school. In the 1897–98 session, there were 9 kindergarten students, 21 in the primary and preparatory departments, 8 in the academic department, and 68 college students.

This photo of the main lecture hall shows dozens of pigtailed and apparently attentive young ladies.

Many NMPC students at the college level were boarders from around Mississippi and the South. A typical dormitory room provided a venue for relaxing with music.

Art was emphasized both for its academic value and as an expressive outlet for NMPC's students.

In 1903, the school's name changed to Mississippi Synodical College (MSC). This class is the elementary section of MSC in the early 1920s; Chesley Smith is second from the left on the back row.

This January 1924 photo shows the underclassmen at MSC seated on the front porch of the original Watson Home; as additions were made to the campus, one of the columns of the old house wound up being incorporated into a cloak room.

This faculty photo of 1924 includes Dr. and Mrs. Robert F. Cooper, directors of MSC from 1920 to 1939. Dr. Cooper was a graduate of Johns Hopkins University and was widely considered an exceptional educator. In spite of his able leadership, MSC was in its final days by the 1930s; enrollment dwindled with the onset of the Depression and more and more women were choosing to study at four-year colleges. Merger with Belhaven College in 1939 brought Mississippi Synodical College's proud history to a finish; only the administration building remains today, housing the Marshall County Historical Museum.

Following the Civil War and Reconstruction, the education of recently freed blacks in Marshall County was a priority. This building was the main structure for the short-lived Baptist Negro College, located east of Salem Bridge.

In 1866, a teachers' college for freed slaves was begun by the Freedman's Aid Society of the Methodist Episcopal Church. Chartered as Shaw University in Holly Springs, it was renamed Rust College in 1890. This unusual building was the original administration building for the college.

The guiding force behind the public school system in Holly Springs was Professor W.A. Anderson, headmaster of Chalmers Institute. The first Holly Springs Public School was built in 1879; the building pictured here appears to be an enlargement of the original structure, which can be seen to the rear. In 1928, this school burned and was replaced by the new Holly Springs High School.

Seated in front of Holly Springs High is the entire student body of 1927—a total of 17 members strong. Chesley Smith is seated, third from the left.

A few years later, when the freshman class of 1930–31 posed, enrollment had risen somewhat.

The same class is pictured two years later, as the junior class of 1932–33. Their number seems to have lessened noticeably. The young man seated on the right of the front row is John Olson, who would survive imprisonment in a Japanese POW camp and the Bataan Death March.

Hundreds of Holly Springs High School graduates had passed through these doors by the time the Class of 1957 sat for its ninth-grade picture. Gus Smith III is seated, third from the left; Hubert McAlexander is in the second row, third from the right.

Six

RELIGION IN
MARSHALL COUNTY

One of the first priorities for the founders of Holly Springs was the establishment of churches. All of the mainstream denominations were represented in the mixture of settlers streaming into the new territory, and they wasted no time in organizing their congregations and initiating plans for places of worship. The Methodist Church assigned three circuit riders to the district, with the intention of serving as many people as possible in the scattered settlements around Marshall County. The Presbyterians were the first to establish a formal body and erect a building, a crude log church which went up in 1836. By 1840, the Methodists, Baptists, and Episcopalians all had buildings in place and active congregations. As their membership and the prosperity of the region grew, newer and more elaborate churchhouses took the place of the original structures. Although several of these churches were used in unforeseen ways during the dark days of the Civil War, the devotion of their parishioners has brought them into the present day as reminders of the deep spiritual commitment of Holly Springs's pioneers.

The Holly Springs Presbyterian Church, the fourth building to serve that congregation, has stood since 1860. Nearly finished in 1861, it was commandeered as a stable and then a munitions storage facility by Union troops. Soldiers used it as target practice; in 1995, Federal-issue lead bullets were found imbedded in the sanctuary floor during renovations. The church was built almost entirely by the labor of members' slaves, and their exceptional artistry is nowhere more evident than in the paneled slave gallery, reached by a flight of narrow circular steps in the octagonal south tower.

The Presbyterian Church was devastated by the Federal occupation. Following the war, Reverend Henry Paine toured the country on a fund-raising drive, soliciting funds from North and South alike to repair and complete the magnificent structure. It was finally finished and dedicated in 1869. This 1894 photo shows the tower still in place; it was destroyed in a storm sometime before 1897, but the supporting arches are still visible in the foyers and attic.

The Holly Springs Methodist Church was built in 1849 to replace a tiny frame structure on Hernando Road. Like the Presbyterian Church, its sanctuary is one floor above street level; originally, this was reached by an outside stair. In 1872, the vestibule and spire were added to bring the church to its present-day appearance and enclose the stair. After the Marshall County Courthouse was accidentally burned in 1864, this church was used as a temporary court site.

This quaint Gothic building was originally Christ Church, serving the Episcopal congregation; in 1857, the Roman Catholic Church purchased it and moved it to East College Avenue, where it stands today. When a new Catholic church opened in 1980, this building was closed; it is now being transformed into a museum.

The Baptists had a churchhouse in service by 1838; this Gothic style building was erected in 1897. After the congregation moved to a larger sanctuary, it was converted into a movie theater.

The first Episcopal services in Holly Springs were held in the courthouse; by 1840, a church had been built on this site, which has been home to the Episcopalians ever since. In 1858, the congregation pledged $9,000 to replace the old building sold to the Catholics, and the existing Christ Church was erected. Its first rector was Joseph Holt Ingraham, an author of religious novels and an architect. In a never-solved incident, he was found dead of a gunshot wound in the vestry of the church in 1860.

This 1900 photo shows the sanctuary of Christ Church; notice the elaborate stenciling along the ceiling and the gas-powered brass chandelier.

In a slightly later photo, the stenciling has been painted over; otherwise the room remains largely unchanged and would be easily recognizable today to a parishioner of that time.

This group of nuns from Kentucky visited the memorial in Hill Crest Cemetery to the Sisters of Charity. After Bethlehem Academy was closed during the yellow fever epidemic of 1878, 12 nuns stayed on in Holly Springs to care for the sick and dying. Six of the twelve sisters died of the disease; in 1879, the community banded together to erect this monument in their memory.

Seven

FORGOTTEN FACES

The photographs which Chesley Smith took personally date back to 1919, when she first acquired a camera and turned it toward the streets and people of her hometown. In later years, she realized the importance of not only recording the daily events and special occasions of Holly Springs, but also the necessity of saving the work of previous generations. She added several extensive collections of nineteenth- and early-twentieth-century photographs to her files; as much as possible, names and dates and locations were noted and recorded. Family albums and formal shots from long-vanished studios were carefully preserved and protected from the disastrous effects of neglect. Some of the subjects in these photos can be identified; others are, at best, educated guesses, and some must be accepted as they are—precious reminders of a time gone by, their names lost in the passage of the years.

Dr. Chesley Daniel, grandfather of Chesley Smith, reads in his office on Market Street. Dr. Daniel was a longtime general practitioner whose first office was in a log cabin east of Holly Springs. Like most of his medical contemporaries, he practiced medicine of every sort, including surgery and obstetrics.

This interior shot of the Bank of Holly Springs shows Mr. Ross, James Fort Daniel, and Henry Craft Fort. Notice the wall calendar advertising buggies.

A picnic for several young couples in the first decade of the 1900s was a closely chaperoned affair. Posing for the camera are Bessie Walters, Robert Masson, Buck Thorne (Chesley Smith's father), Helen Walters, John Pinkston, and Cordelia Leech.

The picnic was held at the Gun Club on Ford's Pond, a popular recreational area south of Holly Springs. It is now part of Wall Doxey State Park.

Baseball was the sports passion of America in the first years of the century, and Holly Springs was no exception. This unidentified team may have been connected with Ole Miss or a semipro group.

Several of the photographs in Chesley Smith's collection are found in an album inherited from her aunt, Lucy Hill Daniel. One displays two unidentified children playing with a very early toy car; note the tiny steering wheel and front tires, which are much smaller than those in the rear.

The "Gibson Girl" hairdos date this photograph to the first decade of the century; the young ladies appear to be much happier about the situation than the overloaded horse.

Harness racing was a popular sport around Mississippi, with many fairgrounds including racetracks.

This unidentified office in Holly Springs shows the more relaxed pace of the business world in bygone days. Notice the two-piece telephone on the elevated desk.

The Masonic Hall on the square was elaborately decorated for a ball honoring Dr. and Mrs. Will Gholson and Dr. and Mrs. Sam Gholson. The second floor of the hall served as the Opera House; later, dances were held there, and at one time it even served as a movie theater.

This playful group is unidentified, as is the large house with wraparound porch. Their dress dates the period to the 1890s or early 1900s.

This water-powered gristmill was likely the one at Ford's Pond, close to the existing lake at Wall Doxey State Park.

These prints from glass negatives likely date to the 1880s or 1890s; sharecropping was the most common form of labor for black families of the time.

Living conditions for many of those in rural Marshall County during this period were dismal at best.

Notice the log base of the chimney with wood comprising the upper half.

In winter, the shutter would be closed over this open window; glass in such houses was practically nonexistent.

Nettie Fant Thompson (second from right) was a noted artist who traveled on the Chatauqua Circuit in the late 1800s. She joined a group of her friends for an upscale occasion in this 1890s shot.

Subjects for glass negative photography were usually carefully posed and required to stand perfectly motionless; this "action" photo is unusually sharp, though damaged by corrosion. In the background of this courthouse square shot can be seen the Masonic Lodge and Blumenthal's Store.

Eight

PEOPLE, PLACES, AND PILGRIMAGES

Thousands of people have called Holly Springs home over the past 160 years. Famous and infamous, noted or notorious, they have all added their own personal touch to the town, each life an enduring footnote to the story of Marshall County. Those who built the first crude houses in the holly grove were, of course, gone long before a camera could record their image for history, but their names echo through generations of descendants who appear in these vintage photographs.

Chesley Smith trained her camera lens on hundreds of Holly Springs natives, recording the everyday and the unusual and, in her own words, "things that wouldn't be here much longer." Her work covers several decades of life in north Mississippi, from the pageantry of homecoming parades and Spring Pilgrimage to the visages of townspeople going about their daily routine. Equally intriguing are the older photos, often dating back a century or more, which she rescued from obscurity. Throughout this collection, the faces and places that meant "home" for several generations of Holly Springs inhabitants are as vibrant as the day the pictures were taken.

This political rally was held at the site of the old fairgrounds, now long since replaced by the Marshall County Industrial Park. Notice the fellow climbing the pole in the background.

Taken on the steps of Walter Place, this photo shows Fredonia Johnson (later Moss) with Nellie the dog, Lillian Walter, Harvey Johnson, Oscar Johnson, and Pearl Walter.

This photo is one of those belonging to Gus Smith Jr.; the ball team is not identified.

Judging by the change in demeanor of the benchwarmers, the game seems to have taken an unpleasant turn for their side.

Sherwood Bonner, a noted writer of Southern dialect stories and close friend and secretary to Henry Wadsworth Longfellow, grew up at Cedarhurst. She returned from Boston to Holly Springs during the 1878 yellow fever epidemic to care for her father and brother, who both died on the same day. Sherwood died of cancer in 1883, at the age of 34.

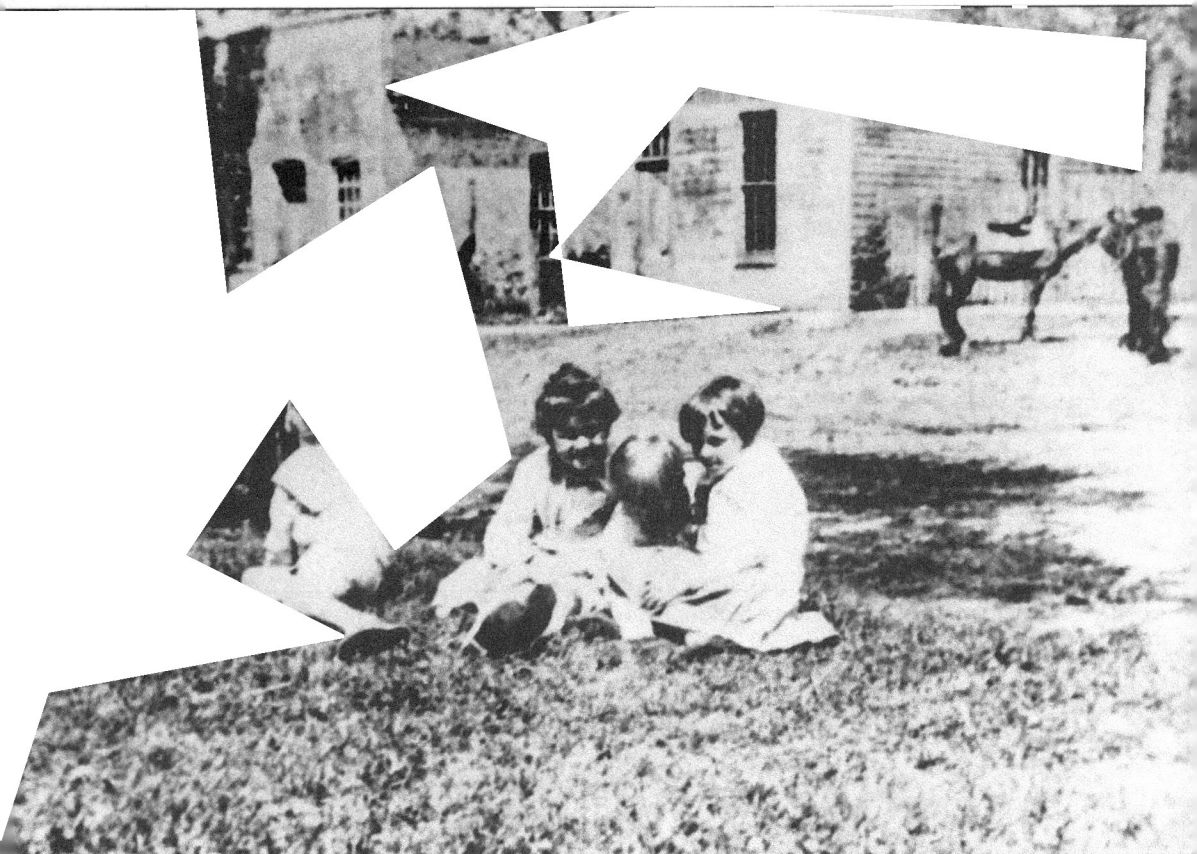

One of the first photographs taken by nine-year-old Chesley Smith in 1919 was this one of children playing on the front lawn of the Presbyterian Church. The shy one on the left was Lytle Rather Jr., who would never face the camera; with him are Tankie Richardson, Pokie Daniel, and Vogy Daniel. Across the street is the building where Mayor A.W. Goodrich died of yellow fever in 1878; to its left is the newspaper office of the Holly Springs *Reporter*.

Oscar Johnson, son-in-law of Colonel Harvey Walter, bought Walter Place in 1917 to use as a vacation home; he had the 20 acres surrounding it landscaped into an elaborate park. Winding roads encircled a shallow lake where local children could swim. Mr. Johnson would bring trainloads of friends from St. Louis for parties in the park.

Ford's Pond was a favorite picnic and fishing spot just a few miles south of Holly Springs; its site is now part of Wall Doxey State Park.

One of the fascinating characters of Holly Springs was Parson Black, a familiar sight on the streets and sidewalks before and during the Depression. Pushing a wheelbarrow, he would scavenge soda bottles, lumps of coal, and stray pieces of wood. He carried a croaker sack in the fall, following behind the cotton wagons and filling his sack with loose bolls. Home was a tiny shack without heat or electricity; when Parson died in 1936, a cigar box with over $13,000 in cash was found tucked under his bed.

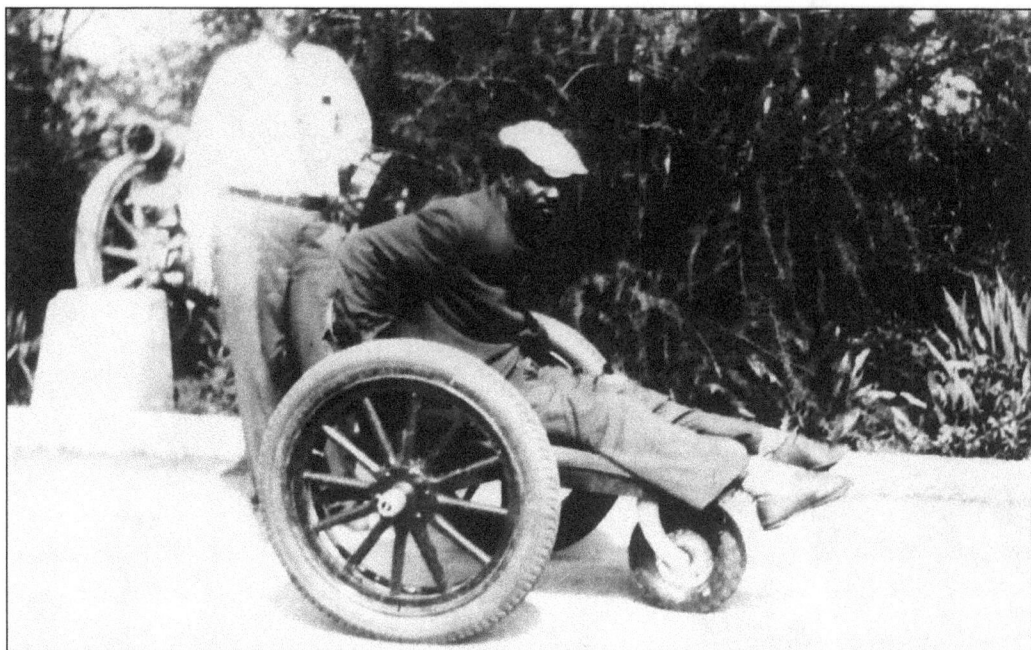

Chesley Smith's stepfather, E.B. Booker, fashioned this wheelchair for a handicapped man out of spare material; the cannon in the background is a World War I–vintage piece which stood on the courthouse lawn for many years.

Strickland Place was an antebellum house with a serpentine walk, its entrance flanked by these two unusual pillars. In this photo, Jimmy Totten and Frank Hopkins appear to be guarding the entrance to the grounds during a 1940s Spring Pilgrimage.

Kate Freeman Clark (right) and her cousins, Cary James Tucker and Sam Gholson, visit in 1950. Miss Clark was a prolific painter who studied with William Chase in New York; upon moving back to Holly Springs, she built a studio onto her house but never produced another painting. Neither did she sell any of her work; at her death, she left the entire collection of over 1,000 paintings to the City of Holly Springs, along with money to build a gallery.

This artist, whose name has been forgotten, spent time at Walter Place doing formal portraits of the family.

"Emmett" was the gardener at Walter Place; it was his job to tend the formal gardens laid out by landscape architects after Oscar Johnson Sr. revitalized the grounds of the old home.

Lucy Mathews Brown and Voorhies Daniel, cousin of Chesley Smith, pose for Chesley's camera in the 1920s.

Martha Smith and an unidentified friend pose in uniform in November 1932. The purpose of the military attire is unclear.

When a rare snowfall blankets the Deep South, all serious business stops and everyone, young and old, joins in the unexpected fun. This January 1940 snow sent Margaret Rather Sullivant, unidentified , Claiborne Rowan Thompson, and Felicia Booker Niven onto College Street for a sled ride.

Since 1936, the highlight of spring in Marshall County has been the annual Pilgrimage tour of homes and churches. Each year, several architecturally and historically significant antebellum homes are open to the public for tours, hosted by their owners and members of the Holly Springs Garden Club. Thousands of visitors from across America make this annual trek and are astonished at the number of beautiful homes and churches in this small town. In this early 1950s photo, Pilgrimage Queen Ann Slayden is surrounded by a large contingent of Governor Hugh White's honorary colonels and Mayor Jim Buchanan.

This 1948 Pilgrimage photo shows Dorothy Seale and Pokie French on the front lawn of the Craft-Fort-Daniel House. Across the street is the small house built by Heber Craft; the site is now occupied by the Marshall County Library.

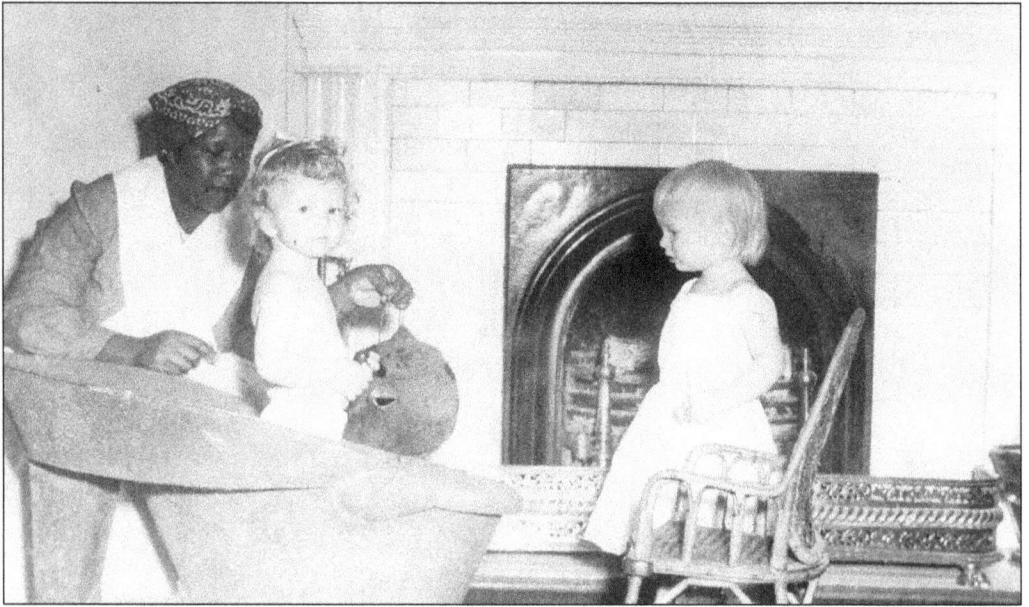

Even the youngest Holly Springs citizens become involved in Pilgrimage activities. In this scenario, long-time Pilgrimage participant Luvenia Driver shows Marie Rather and Vicky Buchanan a tin bathtub and the fireplace used for heating its water at the Dean House.

Polk Place, a frequent inclusion on the Pilgrimage list, was built in 1849 and remodeled by Oscar Johnson Sr., as part of his Johnson Park renovations. Cary Howard Tucker and her sister, Mary Creed, await visitors on the front lawn.

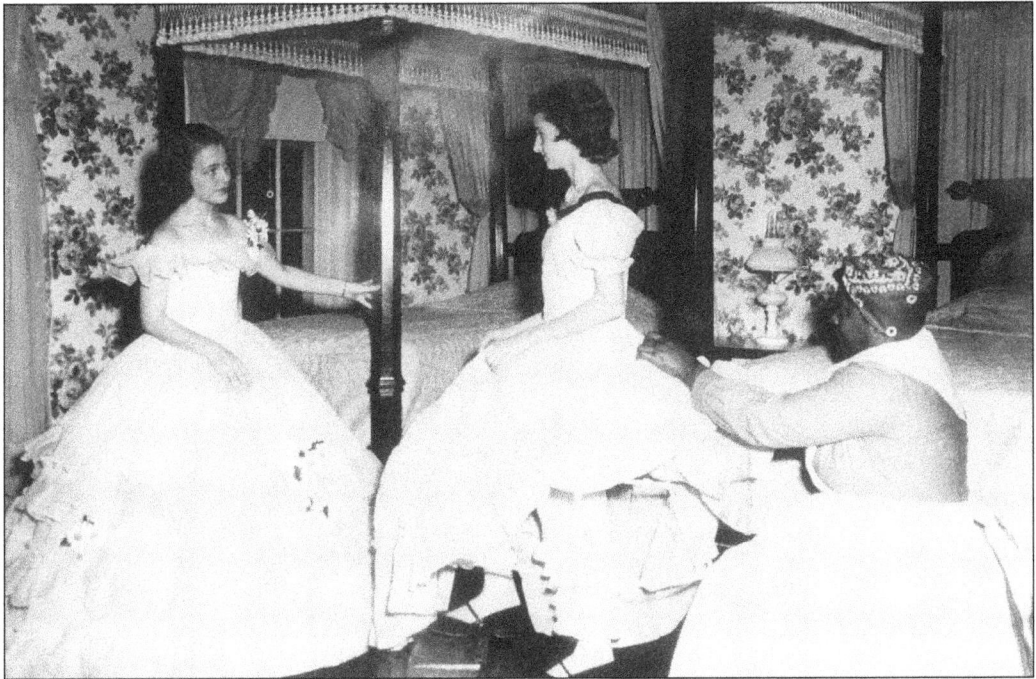

Betty Dale Buford and Michelle Seale are corsetted into their hoopskirts by Luvenia Driver.

One of the early mainstays on the Pilgrimage schedule was Chesley Smith's childhood home, the Craft-Fort-Daniel House. Pokie Daniel stands by the gate which has graced the old home since the 1850s; notice the Native American head design in the ironwork.

In 1948, many Southerners deserted their long-held allegiance to the Democratic Party and its renomination of Harry Truman. They formed the short-lived Dixiecrat Party with Strom Thurmond as their presidential candidate; Mississippi governor Fielding Wright was Thurmond's running mate. This photo shows a group of Mississippi Dixiecrats, including Sidney Hurdle, Tom Stewart, Gus Smith, two unidentified men, Governor Wright, and Reeves Power. Notice the sound equipment on top of the automobile.

The Holly Springs High School cheerleaders for 1951–52 posed for Chesley Smith.

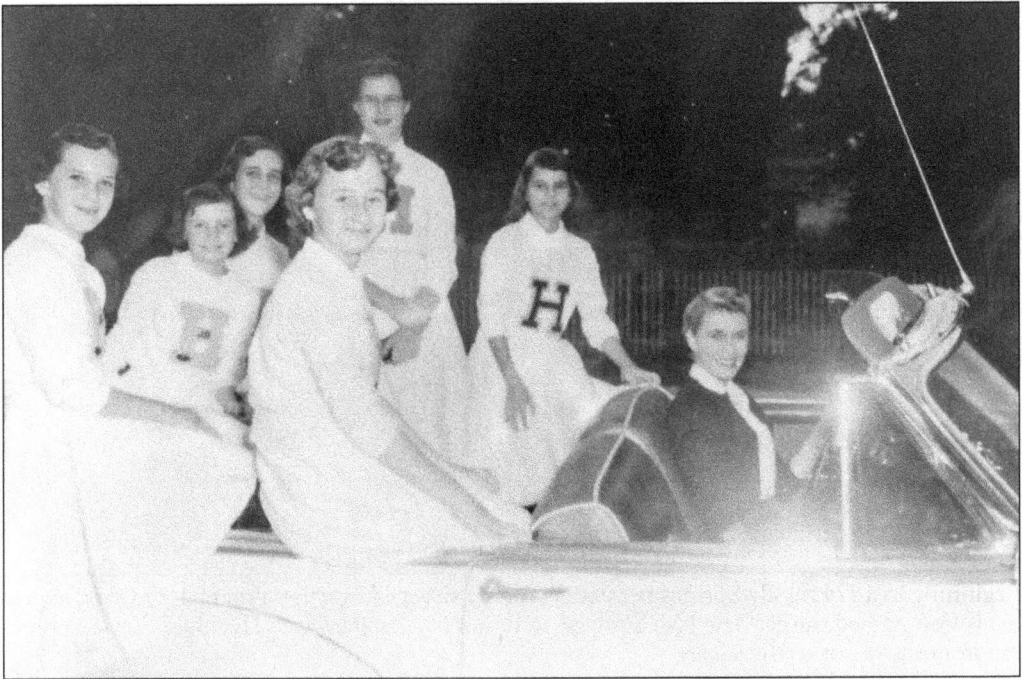

High school activities dominated much of the social calendar of Holly Springs in the years after World War II. Homecoming was an event which involved the entire town.

The annual Homecoming Parade takes a turn around the square; Chesley and Gus Smith's daughter, Caffey, is the homecoming maid seated on the left.

Beginning in 1874, Holly Springs boasted a one-car street railway for a number of years; owner Sam West named the car "the J.M. Scruggs" in honor of a local lawyer. The mule-drawn vehicle ran from the depot to the square.

This small building, just off the square, served as the medical office of Chesley Smith's grandfather, Dr. Chesley Daniel, and also for her brother, Dr. Edward A. Thorne. It was originally built in the 1840s for Dr. Samuel O. Caruthers.

This power plant brought the first electricity to Holly Springs; for many years, electricity was generated only during the night hours. The building, much altered, now serves as a city jail.

This structure was known as "the gas house," generating natural gas power for Holly Springs; it was destroyed in an explosion some years ago.

In most Southern towns, the Confederate monument is located on the courthouse square; Holly Springs's memorial stands in Hillcrest Cemetery. The small cannon on the left side of the base was stolen and never recovered.

Hillcrest Cemetery is one of the most historic burying grounds in Mississippi. Dating back to 1837, the tombstones are carved with the names of most of Holly Springs's founding families. This is the Coxe plot, resting place for the builders of Galena and Airliewood. An unusual feature is the inclusion of a beloved slave; her plot lies at a right angle across the graves of her masters.

Nine

FAMILY AND FRIENDS

If you lived in Holly Springs from the 1920s onward and stood still long enough, chances are that you had your picture taken by Chesley Smith. Her camera focused on everyone and everything in this small Southern town, but most intimately on family and friends. Growing up in a clan whose roots stretched back to the first days of Marshall County, cousins and aunts and uncles were abundant and ready material for the lens of an observant photographer. Friends posed for informal snapshots and, in the process, wonderful old buildings and street scenes are frozen in the backgrounds. Tin Lizzies, dirt roads, and the simple games of another time are treasures preserved on film.

In addition to her own extensive portfolio of photos, Mrs. Smith became the keeper of the family's albums and the youthful pictures of her husband, Gus Smith Jr. With such an extended network of sources, her collection touches on almost every corner of life in Holly Springs during the twentieth century.

Edward Alston Thorne and Chesley Thorne were born to Voorhies Daniel and Buxton Thorne; their mother's family could be traced back to the first settlers of Holly Springs, while their father was a native of North Carolina.

This pre-1910 photo shows young Edward Thorne and his sister, Frances (1908–1910), with an unidentified playmate.

Chesley sits with her favorite doll, Belle, by "the Pit." This structure behind the Craft-Fort-Daniel House extended several feet into the ground and had glass panes on its south face; delicate plants were stored there through the winter and it furnished a wonderful place to play.

In this 1912 photo, Corrinne Butler, Janie Mack Lyon, and Edward Thorne play in front of a house on Gholson Street. This home had a sidewalk paved with inverted clay beer bottles, making an interesting pattern of brown and black circles along its length.

Gus Smith Jr. and Glenn Fant grew up together and remained best friends throughout their lives. Baseball gave way to college years, wartime service, and careers in law, but the friendship endured for nine decades.

Gus Smith Jr. was born in 1904; his great-grandfather was General A.M. West, owner of Oakleigh in the years following the Civil War. In this 1912 photo, young Gus poses in full Native American regalia with his sister, Louise Caffey Smith.

Native American dress was obviously an enduring style for Holly Springs children in the first years of the twentieth century. A large group gathered for Gus's eighth birthday party in 1912.

The War in Europe did not directly affect small-town Mississippi until American troops became involved in 1917, but its devastation and tragedy was well known even in this corner of the world. Soldiers camped out near Salem Bridge, and the women of Holly Springs rolled bandages to be sent overseas. Each night, the power company would shut down for one minute and the town would go dark as an indication that this was a time to pray for the soldiers in Europe. In this 1917 photo, Margaret Rather and Chesley Thorne are posed in their Red Cross nurses' uniforms in front of the Gholson House.

Chesley and Edward Thorne's father, Buxton Thorne, died shortly before Chesley's birth. Their mother, Voorhies Daniel Thorne, married Ed Booker (known to the children as "Bookie") in 1918, when Chesley was almost eight. He owned a hardware store on the square and also ran a wholesale oil and gasoline business.

Edward Thorne was often the subject of his sister's photographs; his interest in sports is evident in this photograph.

In 1920, Edward Thorne and Juanita Sudduth posed for Chesley on the front lawn of the Presbyterian Church. Juanita went on to serve in the Women's Army Corps, commanding the first unit of this group in the Philippines during World War II.

Snookums the pony spent the summer of 1921 with Chesley Smith's family; the horse was blind in her right eye and would only make left turns, which made riding around the block a one-way affair. Here, Walker Sudduth and Edward Thorne enjoy a double ride. Notice the tower of the Presbyterian Church in the background.

Pokie Daniel and Bessie Mulcahy pose by one of Holly Springs's early cars in 1919. At the time, all the streets were dirt; gravel and asphalt were still several years away. The arrival of more automobiles caused a tremendous dust problem and the streets were watered each day.

Chesley and the Finley sisters pose by the Finley's Franklin auto en route to Biloxi in 1922.

Edward Thorne proudly sports a pipe and cowboy hat in front of the Craft-Fort-Daniel House.

During her teen years, Chesley was an avid rider. She is pictured here with Dolly, a favorite horse.

After two years at Mississippi Synodical College, Chesley attended Randolph-Macon College in Lynchburg, Virginia, from 1929–1930. Elizabeth Baker of Collierville, Tennessee, was a classmate there during that time, and has remained a friend of Chesley's through the years.

After the death of Chesley's grandmother, Fannie Fort Daniel, her aunts decided the 90-year-old Craft-Fort-Daniel House needed a thorough cleaning. All the contents of the house were dragged onto the back lawn for dusting, discarding, or burning, directed here by Aunt Sallie May Daniel. Chesley managed to salvage several of her great-grandfather's books and journals from the rubbish heap. Notice the large pie safe in the background; it probably did not survive the day.

Memphis has long been the preferred day trip and shopping mecca for Marshall Countians. Before the days of suburban malls, ladies would dress in their best and stroll the streets downtown to shop at Goldsmith's and Lowenstein's department stores. In 1938, Chesley's mother, Voorhies Booker, and her friend Ruth Finley joined the parade of shoppers on Main Street.

In December 1931, Chesley Thorne married Lemuel Augustus Smith Jr., known to all as Gus. He was a successful young lawyer with a future that would take him to a seat on the Mississippi Supreme Court. Marrying Chesley, of course, meant that the photographs of his youth and college days would be merged with her rapidly expanding collection and preserved for future generations. Here, Paul Blount, Gus, Katherine Henderson, and Bob Barner practice for a University of Mississippi theatrical production.

The summer of 1925 was a time for tennis for the young bachelors of Holly Springs; David Groskind, Bill Howard, Gus, and Glenn Fant posed for a post-game photo.

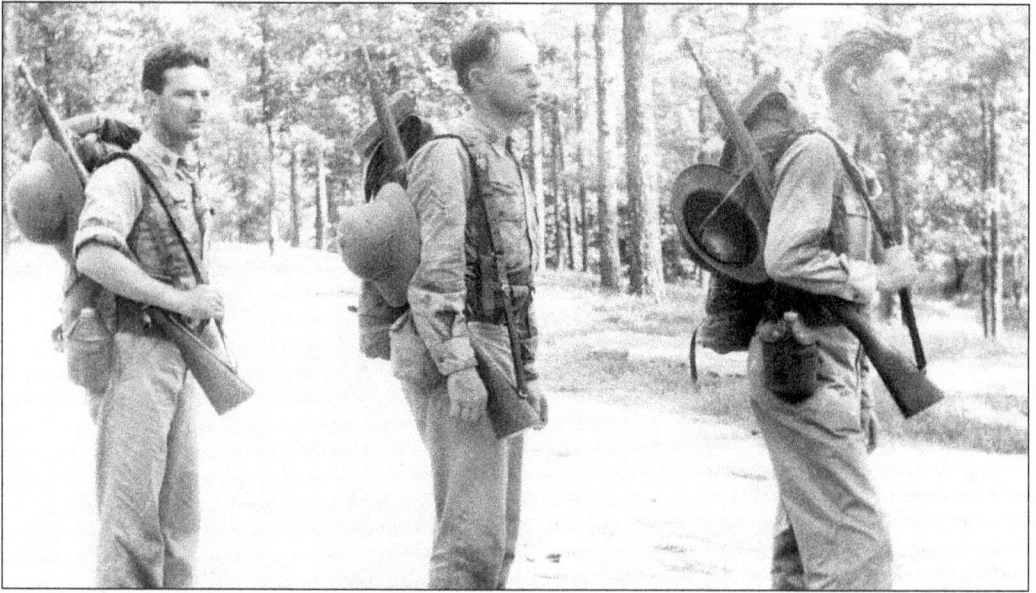

World War II took many of the men of Marshall County into the service, including Gus Smith. In preparation for their impending induction, Gus, Glenn Fant, and George Buchanan undertook a 16-mile hike at a Civilian Military Training Camp in Alabama. Gus went on to serve as a lieutenant commander in the Navy for three years.

Chesley and Gus Smith have always been actively involved in all aspects of life in their hometown; Chesley returned to Ole Miss for her B.A.E. in mathematics in the late 1950s and taught for many years at Holly Springs High School. Gus served as president of the school board and is pictured here with Norman B. McKenzie Sr., longtime superintendent of the Holly Springs schools.

126

After a long and successful career practicing law, Gus Smith was appointed to the Supreme Court of Mississippi in 1965; he served with distinction in that position until 1982. He is seated on the right in this photo of the court.

Throughout this collection of photographs runs threads of family and friends, relationships maintained and nurtured across decades of change and challenge. The children seen here, captured on film while picnicking at a sand ditch near Holly Springs, reappear in Chesley Smith's photographs years later as adults. Such is the enduring fabric of life in this corner of Mississippi, a legacy preserved for generations yet to come by the foresight of one remarkable woman.

www.ingramcontent.com/pod-product-compliance
Lightning Source LLC
Chambersburg PA
CBHW080902100426
42812CB00007B/2122